TRINITY

TRINITY

Poems by Susan Ludvigson

LOUISIANA STATE UNIVERSITY PRESS
Baton Rouge and London
1996

Designer: Michele Myatt
Typefaces: Serlio, Adobe Garamond
Typesetter: Impressions Book and Journal Services, Inc.
Printer and binder: Thomson-Shore, Inc.

Library of Congress Cataloging-in-Publication Data
Ludvigson, Susan.
    Trinity : poems / by Susan Ludvigson.
      p. cm.
    ISBN 0-8071-2115-0 (alk. paper). — ISBN 0-8071-2116-9 (pbk. :
alk. paper)
    I. Title.
    PS3562.U27T7   1996
    811'.54—dc20   96-9573
                                                                         CIP

Grateful acknowledgment is made to the editors of the following periodicals, where some of the poems in this collection originally appeared: *American Voice:* "Daughter, why do you keep" (No. 37, 1995), "Every day you advance a little" (No. 37, 1995), "I know what you want to believe" (No. 37, 1995), "Nothing is as it was" (No. 37, 1995), "What do you tell yourself" (No. 37, 1995); *Gettysburg Review:* "The Gospel According to Mary Magdalene" (Autumn, 1995); *Pagagonian Winds:* "So it begins, the long days fringed" (Spring, 1996), "You think I am never alone" (Spring, 1996); *Poet Lore:* "Today someone asks you" (Spring, 1996), "Why, when I speak to myself" (Spring, 1996), "You know the trees sing differently" (Spring, 1996), *The Review:* "Do I understand you right?" (Fall, 1995), "In school you lean over a microscope" (Fall, 1995); *Southern Humanities Review:* "Consider how the moment enters itself" (Spring, 1996), "I know it is meant for me" (Spring, 1996), "I see that you've entered" (Spring, 1996), "You honor your father" (Spring, 1996); *Southern Review:* "In the Abiding Dark" (Summer, 1996), "Now your mother sleeps while you" under the title "God Speaks to Emily Dickinson About Her Absent Father" (Autumn, 1994), "What do you think it means" under the title "God Speaks to Emily Dickinson About Her Dreams" (Autumn, 1994).

The paper in this book meets the guidelines for permanence and durability of the Committee on Production Guidelines for Book Longevity of the Council on Library Resources. ∞

For Joel Bartels and Scott Ely

CONTENTS

I

I

THE GOSPEL ACCORDING TO MARY MAGDALENE

On the subjects of which we know nothing, we both believe and disbelieve a hundred times an Hour, which keeps Believing nimble.

—Emily Dickinson

1 / THE CASTING OUT
OF THE SEVEN DEVILS

Lord, I said to him, I sin.
What moves me to answer the flesh

when spirit calls in its light
and singular tones?

A well-made man is never invisible
to me, even beneath heavy cloaks.

Sometimes, as morning gathers toward heat,
a man's arm brushes mine in the market.

Then a bolt shoots through me like lightning,
the scent of earth rising around me.

What is this trembling, why does the wind
itself become dark breath on my skin?

I asked him these things.
I did not tell him that he

made my nights a desert where stars
were so bright they drilled into me

lying alone on the dunes. My kind of longing
was not his command.

I meant to do his bidding, though what he bade
passed through me like music.

Woman, he told me, *I know you well.*
Though devils spin you through lives

you cannot and do not wish in your blood
to forget, they are a gang of thieves

who will, if we don't throw them out,
take the gold and the silver

your heart would leave
on my father's altar. They will strip

your walls bare where now
you delight your wakings with silk.

The rugs piled soft for your bed
will be rolled up and carried away.

These thieves will make you believe
the house of your body is aflame

and take everything
in the name of rescue.

Cast them out, Lord, I prayed.
Let me come to you rich with treasures.

His eyes described my being.
He took me by my shoulders, his hands

lifted me, and I felt the devils depart
all at once, my head in sudden pain

that left me so weak, I fell back
to my knees, weeping.

Mary, he said, so softly
I barely heard him. *Mary,*

as his hands stroked my hair,
as his hands stroked and stroked my hair.

2 / THE ANOINTING

I arrived at the house of Simon, a Pharisee.
My master sat at his table, red wine

and lamb before him, the fresh meat
steaming, the fragrance of olive oil

a perfume of gold in the air.
I could not help myself, I began

to weep. I knelt before my lord
and let my tears fall, washing his dusty feet

in that overflow of rapture,
then dried them with my hair.

I could not speak, for his presence
stopped my words

as if they were stunned
with drink. I drew a small box

from inside my robe.
Opening its alabaster lid,

I poured ointment over those feet
while even the dove in the window

grew silent. Jesus loved
my penitence first,

then the way my hair fell
to the floor, its weight against his skin.

I kissed my lord's ankles
as if Simon were not in the room,

as if the other guests were not
exchanging glances.

Jesus laid his hand on my hand,
spoke to Simon and the others:

Try to understand, he said.
I have come for her as well.

My father never
blinded me to beauty.

She is a flame whose light
burns whiter now that I am here.

And I? Look into my eyes,
black with awakening.

Even I must learn my way
by trial and touch.

The dove flew to my shoulder.
I felt its body hesitate, the tremolo of wings.

When the men spoke again,
only the voice of Jesus

entered my ear. I did not hear
meaning. It was like my own heart

beating wild, the sea
pulsing in, the tide rising.

3 / The Wedding at Cana

I welcomed his mother into my arms.
Still young, she commanded her son

in a voice he sometimes rebuked, but she
would have her say. Though the servants

were mine, she ordered the feast—
goat cooked with mint and pears, spiced breads,

doves wrapped in grape leaves, baked in wine,
figs, an array of honeyed cakes,

and more. She saw to the cloths spread
on tables, hung branches over the doors.

She perfumed the house with incense and cedars,
that fragrance wafting to my room

where a girl brushed my hair,
braided it with lavender. Why was I afraid?

Bridegroom, I wanted to cry, to call him
to me. But he was welcoming guests

from Nazareth and from Capernaum,
from Magdala, my village, and from Gennesaret.

There were those who traveled even from Hebron
and Bethlehem, and from Arimathea.

When I came out, some of the faces turned dark,
like poplar leaves in sudden wind.

So many, I could not recognize friends.
Bodies pressed back, making a path

for me through my house, now unfamiliar
as a foreign temple. But he took my hand,

and when the vows were said, my heart lifted
and was glad. Then his mother whispered

that the wine was nearly gone.
She called the servants. Jesus said,

Fill all the jars with water. When
they returned, it was wine.

Love, I said to him, I was water,
flowing over banks, flooding fields

already wet from too much rain.
You contained me. You changed me.

Which is the greater miracle?
More gently than I had heard her,

his mother answered: He is the vine.
This is all we must remember.

4 / THE CRUCIFIXION

I was afraid. My fear was so great
the doves would not come to me,

though I stood in a circle of crumbs,
arms extended, hands filled with bread.

I did not go into the hall
where the men ate their last feast together.

My lord had instructed me to prepare the tomb,
to lay clean cloths on a boulder,

to leave a jug of water there.
Trust my heart, he said.

It has been tested.
My father wishes me to die

and not to die.
Each morning I give myself

to the dust of the road,
each night to the dark and to you

whose lips chart
my still unbroken flesh.

It is written, he said,
his pulse changing. *I must go.*

That night I watched the moon
cross over the garden,

the moon with its placid
face, gliding as if through water,

as if it were breathing through water.
I wanted to absorb its white, cast

into the trees like hope,
or to be absorbed.

When I was with him, I believed.
My heart's wings grew quiet. But away

from his hungry body, that body singing
its clear, sharp note into the cedars,

I lost faith in the fragile plan.
There in Gethsemane, I tried to pray.

Nothing. Nothing but the rustling
of leaves, then a cloud racing to obscure

the moon, so that the garden fell
into heavy shadow, animals stalked

the paths. A wind came up fast.
Limbs torn from the olive trees

were cast on the ground. I ran, shaken,
to my brother's house. When Jesus entered

my chamber late with a lamp, I saw the bones
in his face, the wells under his eyes.

We did not speak.
All night, we were one voice.

I could not watch them scourge him,
though I heard the lashes

split the parched air,
heard the tearing of his skin.

I could not follow close
as he staggered under the weight

on his bloodied back.
From a distance, I saw him stumble.

Lord, Lord, I cried, what will become of us?
I was ashamed,

thinking of myself. I stood at the edge
of the crowd as they drove the nails.

Too far away to hear his groans, yet
they filled my throat, seemed wrenched

from my mouth. When the cross was raised,
I fell to the ground, lay there, I think, for hours,

while the crowd, restless, drank wine from skins,
stepped over me, laughing.

I could not urge my spirit
or my eyes to rise.

At last, a shout went up. I raised my head,
saw a cup lifted to his lips.

Not vinegar, as some reported later,
but something to make him sleep

a drowning sleep, a sleep
so close to death he'd feel

the water closing over him,
his breath dissolving

under waves of dream.
Oh, that he might survive—

but if the measure were wrong, the dream
would end, and—more mercifully—he'd die.

My love's head fell forward.
It was over.

They took him down. I struggled up.
Someone helped me walk.

After that, I don't remember.
In my brother's house, I slept

until he woke me. Go, he said. Jesus is waiting.
I went to the tomb, my heart beating double.

I waited until the stone rolled back. Two men
in white attended him, two Essenes. They motioned me

to come in. My kisses
were balm, my lord said, and would renew him.

I pressed my mouth to his mouth,
to his eyelids, then to his wounds.

His mother came in, and other women.
We carried him out into the sun,

which fell in rings
all around him.

5 / The Flight into Gaul

In my brother's house we passed an anxious week.
The two Essenes stayed,

their white robes flowing quiet
through the rooms. They took turns standing watch

inside his door, those guardian angels. The rest
of us—me, his mother Mary, and my brother—

sat *shiva*. When guests came,
grief was not hard to feign in our exhaustion

and our fear. When we were alone, we gathered
grapes, salted lamb, put by a few clean robes.

From time to time, my husband woke in fever,
not himself, shouting curses

mixed with prayers. He implored—
How many chambers

must I enter, Father?
The wolves of darkness devour me!

What flies in at the window?
What beats its black body against the walls?

What drums against the air?
He covered his ears

against what he heard,
and I could not persuade him

of the silence. At last his brow
grew cool again, he asked for water.

On the day the Essenes proclaimed him well
enough to travel, we filled the skins

with water, packed bread and blankets.
By camel, by starlight, we traveled

to the sea, where my brother had arranged
our passage. The boatman did not know us,

thought us poor, glad to trade a simple fare
for the camels. He told us to be patient

while he led them
to a stable in the distance.

Half a day we wasted, waiting for that man
to amble back. None of us was calm.

Jesus stayed in the shadows, watched the sky,
his eyes ringed dark. I paced

beneath the plane trees,
keeping watch for passersby who might recognize

my lord. By noon, the air was still.
No leaf shimmered green to silver.

The few clouds maintained
their languid shapes. I fed my husband raisins.

His mother frowned when he took my fingers
in his mouth. I felt a shiver in my womb.

By then, the water was so calm
I could see my face reflected, swollen.

At last, my brother pushed us off,
the craft heavy with the five of us.

The boatman, old enough to be my father,
rowed with the strength of two young men.

Our destination was Narbonne, a settlement
of Jews where we might live.

6 / THE BRANCHING

Between the pains, I remembered
the words of my lord:

The body, miraculous, rises
on blue wings, rises

out of agony and stupor so quickly
it's hard to remember the dark

paths of its going. It rises
shivering, then warms to stillness.

The body does not believe
in words, but in updrafts of air,

impossible transformations,
sun surrounding it, the whole skin shining.

Between the pains, I panted these words
and other litanies: Abraham was father

to Isaac, who was father to Jacob,
who was father to Judas.

I said the names, the charms
of the names, up to Matthan, who was father

to Jacob, who was father to Joseph,
the husband of Mary

of whom was born Jesus the Nazarene,
my husband, who came to be called Christ.

And Jesus, I murmured, is father to the child
who will be born here

in the city of Narbonne, in Gaul,
of me, Mary the Magdalene.

Lord, I cried to my husband, I am riven,
I will be delivered not of devils now, but of the son

of the son of kings. Flesh is made holy
in us. Once more and once more I cried

as the pains came faster. Mary
his mother laid cool cloths on my brow.

Let us follow rivers back to their source, I whispered.
Let us cross white mountains into paradise,

into the promised land of the spirit.
Jesus prayed outside the room. He heard,

he listened to my words, my pleas.
He said, *Yes, we will go*

inland. We will enter new lands,
my kingdom will be vast, unending.

When it was finished, I rested, I slept.
I saw my image carved

in marble, with a child.
I dreamed my husband's mouth

at my breast, woke to the infant Benjamin
suckling, the vine branching, the changed world.

II

LETTERS BACK
God Responds to Emily Dickinson

Unless we become as Rogues, we cannot enter the kingdom of heaven.
—Emily Dickinson, in a letter to Dr. Holland

In school you lean over a microscope,
astonished by revelations
under glass, such minute clarity
controlled.

I tell you, child, there is more power
in the way your mind brings matter
into focus and recombines the elements,
more beauty infused in the world
by your naked eye.

You think you want congruence,
our imaginations closer
than the rings of Saturn,
yours just enclosed in mine.

Let it be enough that a few things
are predictable. You know
when you can peaches
your mother's mood
becomes a wren.

Let your will resist me,
the future be the sky you'll map,
heaven visible like stars
when they are.

What do you think it means
that you dream of your father's house
flooding, that solid brick lifted
from its moorings, the whole
house floating east, toward the center
of Amherst? I know it puzzles you
that sometimes you are inside
looking down the stairs to the hall
where nobody hears you calling
for Vinnie, who may be trapped
in the kitchen. You watch in fascination
as your mother's prize side table
floats toward the door and out,
as the carpets lift from the floors,
promising next to be airborne.
Sometimes you're walking back
from shopping in the village
when you see the house
coming toward you, its grace not lost
in its drift from one side
of the watery street to the other.
Your father in the doorway
waves as if you were a guest
coming late for dinner, as if it's he
who's moving toward an unfathomed future.
Either way, you are not frightened.
And when you wake, you feel
that you know what the others
don't know, though you cannot
explain it. Let me tell you
this much: when in the morning
you put a finger into the garden's

April soil, the earth
will be soft and damp. You'll soon
name its richness desire.

Now your mother sleeps while you
gather the minutes between one form
of tending and another
to write prayers. Your father
away again, she is all yours,
burden and pleasure, like a garden.
You wonder how men imagine the world—
the invisible polishing of furniture,
the way meals appear,
loaves and fishes to be blessed.
You, ghostlike, deliberately
not holy, float to your mother's room
with a tray, hoping he'll ask
after your health on his return.
Sometimes I fear you listen for my voice
in his: distracted, not knowing
what he does not want to hear.

You know the trees sing differently
for you, full of minor chords.
It's true, most who pass under that shelf
of elms hear something that doesn't rhyme
but blends to a plain sweetness.

There is less to quicken the pulse
in other people's nights
than in your noons, when everything turns
toward imbalance. What I love is that

you love that tilt, however you lament,
and fill it with a consequence the others miss—
and that you hear dissonance
under the cardinal's call.

Daughter, why do you keep
demanding miracles? Even I
cannot stop what's started.
When your aunt coughs blood,
it's not my face
in the branches of the oak.
I mourn as you do, for the earth
has got away from me.

I want you to find these notes
dropped into your lap, these
turning leaves. Yes,
I see your anger.
You will not leave it
at the doorstep
as you intend.

You honor your father,
letting him think you
merely clever, womanly.
He will never guess
you are oak
disguised as willow.

Genius webs the world
beneath its surfaces.
When you enter
the other life
your roots will branch
through Massachusetts
and the country, and even
beyond the country.

Already the tapestries you weave
are attaching themselves
to rock and clay,
to riverbeds and the furrows
beneath mountains.

Every day you advance a little
toward me, some hours so long
you name them pain, eternity arrived
in its coarsest form, an ache
so immense you are all muscle, enclosed
in nothing greater than your skin.

Sometimes the opposite—a man
comes to the house, his brown hat
twirled on a fingertip, voice
calling up the stairs, your name
ringing through the hallway.
Then all your refusals to come down
are like the tablecloth
you took off this morning
and dropped in a heap,
though the swirls of naked wood
made you rush for another white cover.
The day disappears like a bowl of oranges
set before children.

As you rock yourself through the night,
you forget me altogether. It's all right.
You'll wake with his name alive
on the April air coming bright
through the window, and your breath
will still be mine.

I know what you want to believe—
that if he should come in the night
and you, innocent as dream,
welcome him, sleep so heavy
on your skin you can't distinguish
it from his, the world would
change shape, change substance.
As dawn arrived,
his body would polish yours
to a light so blinding
both must become pure soul.
The way you imagine his wife
transformed to dew
evaporating in the morning sun,
nothing left to say she'd even been.

Do I understand you right?
Sometimes even I can get confused,
hear things nobody says, your voice
a plaint that might be lost birds
or wind. What if his wife died,
what if suddenly she was no more
the screen through which you see
each other, softened by that barrier?
You think it's what you want.
When it happens, it will not have been
desire, nor my reluctant answer.
But you will know the desolation then
of wishes realized, and terror.
He'll be so present you'll think
the house is filled with him,
his voice, his bearing larger
than any man's who's ever crossed
your threshold. His face
will fill every window,
and nights, no stars will shine.
Your pen will be as idle
as your neighbors' tongues
if he takes you away, her house
vaster than all the rooms
of your mind, and filled
with furniture you could not abide.

So it begins, the long days fringed
in gold. These are the ones you wait for,
pink sky reminding you of Italian Alps
you will never see. And yet you think this
is happiness, the simplicity of bodies
imagined against that landscape.

It's a land where body once loomed
like a star in the firmament.
Now the color of flesh is background,
absent of figure.

You could almost forget the soul
lingering by the shore of a diminished lake,
hidden in dark folds of earth.

What do you need? What does anyone need?
The cell of darkness is there, it takes over
the evening hills, growing and growing,
your heart lost in it.

Consider how the moment enters itself
when you're not looking, scarcely
paying attention, imagination
trusting what comes
on the surrounding air, sweet
or cool, whatever wafts
through. Your whole body
participates, yet, as in dream,
hardly moves, nearly
paralyzed with pleasure.
How you are taken into and out of
yourself at once, language
a braid, unbraiding, so that
what the fairy tales call tresses
loosen in your hands, brushing
your eyes back to time,
that slow surprise.

Look at you. A careless stranger
or the postman might think you mad,
staring into the clover, your hair
loose around your shoulders.
You forget yourself. Oh, I tolerate
too much impudence, the way you whirl
around me as if I were a canna
and you a hummingbird, quick
and innocent as earliest Eden.
There is history still
to be made. Try to remember
that even as your eyes fail,
my sight penetrates each particle
of the earth, each trumpet vine
and snail, each parlor where a soul,
in its pride, thinks itself alone.

To a new friend you write,
"To multiply the harbors
does not reduce the sea."
Why do you not find
the only harbor there is?
No, you're perverse, inclined
to let your words
scatter like bread
over the waters,
and then to think
they'll transform themselves
to inlets and coves
the heart of anyone
might row to.
No, I am not jealous.
I want, simply, for you
to be original *and* mine,
not turn to me late
as to any port.

Nothing is as it was.
Remember girlhood's promises?
Last week you saw the light
as pins descending
through nearly impassable clouds,
slow as hours spent at a bedside,
no heat when they arrived.

You know all the might-have-beens
by heart. But when
your brother's child stops circling
the house, his kite limp
in the hallway, grief weighs you
to your bed. Admit he was not,
should not have been, yours.
You have chosen well, and I am here
to watch you save yourself.

We are not keepers of the treasure,
you and I. Your job is to celebrate,
not hold. Everything will pass
through your fingers or your mind.
It will be like waking into a room
so vast, the world of objects and desires
will be contained there: music, gold,
dandelions, books, delicate china,
rifles, cats of every color, men
with smooth muscles, men
with beards, day lilies, walnut chairs.
You will sift them as the light
pours through like sand. What lasts
is what amazement finds in every common place,
all the heart can and cannot resist.

"Not possible," you cry
when you hear the news.
You who have seen death
narrow the body to a rod,
stem of drying willow, less
and less supple branch.
You know everything
is possible, and yet
when you hear that the wife,
after all these months
of grieving him, is ill
with a different darkness,
you say it can't be true.
Child, though you have
no names for it yet,
though names will wait
another century, your heart
has always known
these truths. The body
does not want me, does not
want to see me face to face.
But the spirit of that woman
has yearned for me all her life.
She buries it every fall
like a bulb, hoping
that if it returns
it will burst to something
bright as tulip, hoping
equally that it will not
come up, will dissolve
back into the earth
where it never has to breathe
again. Neither has happened

before. Always the shoots
rise into April, and her own
heavy boot walks over it,
over and over, until
it exhausts itself,
alive, but nothing opening.

What do you tell yourself
when dreams skitter away
like rabbits, any gesture
enough to set them running?

You say you listen for me
later in the garden,
sometimes hear
the whisper of the dill,
but not my voice.

Today I came before first light
to sit with you, watching
your closed eyes flutter.
What passed through you then
was a procession. I was one
of the mourners, disguised,
who held out his hand.
You kept your head down,
did not look at my face
but put coins in my palm
as if I were the beggar.

Why, when I speak to myself,
do I so often think of you?
You've hardly seen the world,
while I contain it. And yet
when my net flies out, settles
in a hush over the river,
you're the one who never
feels trapped, who knows
how to weave
in and out of that mesh.

I like having you on the earth,
a reminder that what I give there,
so often misconstrued, is felt
in one who could not be my wife
or sister, but walks
the labyrinth of my love
as if she had a map.

Daughter, you need not
say anything. I know
how you stumble back
and forth to the garden,
not seeing the lilies
swaying, not seeing
hollyhocks or ligularia,
though you planted them,
then weeded every morning
before breakfast. Now,
you might as well be blind.

You will recover.
Color will impress itself
on your skin again—
petals and leaves
will fall to your face
and shoulders, and you
will close your eyes
from too much pleasure.

But it will not happen
in a season. I see
the words, still frozen
in your pen, the hand
remembering only February.

That's where you will find
me, though you have stopped
looking, though you think
you will not look again.

What happens when only fragments
drift through the scrim of dawn,
nothing you can name?
These months, your shuttered
dreams seem designed
to keep me out. Am I a longing,
or a plague? When I drift
through your nights, you hear
dry wind against the pane.
Have you meant to give me
your desolation? Do you believe
I can carry anything
and not feel the weight?

I see that you've entered
the amber world again.
Though you try not to see me,
I am also there. I appear
in the view from every window,
not heaviness but hue.

Alone in your Amherst room,
you watch another country open.
How the sky changes.
How mountains rise up,
pinnacles to be scaled.
And on the other side,
olive trees, bougainvillea.
Refusing to find me there,
your skin darkens and plumps,
something lets go.

I know it is meant for me,
this new sign of impatience—
ripping up the mint and the daisies,
suddenly hating prolixity
and how the seasons
increase their demands.
So today you court endings again.

You think you listen for me,
but it's your own will
you hear. It pounds in your ears
like rain against rock.
It reminds you that you choose,
over and over, to till
one plot, small, obdurate.

Today someone asks you
to define the soul.
It is what remains, you say,
when strength has left
the arms, when the muscles
are too fatigued to remember
their old grace.
It is what remains,
though no one can guarantee
that its wings are not like arms.
No one can say for certain
that it will carry itself
out the doors of the body
and back to its home.
It is a sparrow, you say,
sometimes weighted with ice.

But I tell you, it is not
a sparrow. The soul is a hawk.
It makes shadows ripple over
the earth. It writes boldly
against the light, its form solid
in what you claim is flimsy air.

You think I am never alone.
In one sense it's true—
the world, so much a part
of me, so much my own,
cannot allow my absence.

I sometimes stand back, away,
but it's as if you, dreaming,
had set yourself down
in the South.

Waking, you'd be blinded by dogwood
brushing whole branches
against your window.

Human voices might drift
somewhere beyond or behind you,
but your mind would be
so filled with white,
you'd hear and not hear them.

In fact, this is aloneness
having nothing to do
with geography.

When you are most yourself,
which is to say, most estranged,
I am there, in the room,
equally removed.

III

IN THE ABIDING DARK

Oh, Sir, may one eat of hell fire with impunity here?
> —Emily Dickinson's remark at a dinner
> where flaming plum pudding was served

She prayed, and her prayer was monstrous because in it there was no margin left for damnation or forgiveness, for praise or for blame—those who cannot conceive a bargain cannot be saved or damned.
> —Djuna Barnes, *Nightwood*

Every man and every artist, whether he is Nietzsche or Cézanne, climbs each step in the tower of his perfection by fighting his duende, not his angel, as has been said, nor his muse. This distinction is fundamental, at the very root of the work.
> —Federico García Lorca

1

We know that everything comes down to choice.
One night I find myself at a party,
critics yelling at each other, ice

rattling in their glasses like sabers—an arty
gathering, all the duels safely verbal.
I do not join any argument. My body

becomes the antagonist: I hear there's a ball
being held downstairs. "You can't go there,"
one of the critics says. "Only men are allowed."

He bars the door. The others stare
in disapproval as I slip past the barrier
of his arms. I descend the stairs

into a room where women are carried
naked into other rooms and to shadowed corners,
where couples are coupling everywhere

I look: women embrace women, men fornicate
with anyone in reach. The light is smoky,
someone makes a joke. The word *foreigners*

hovers on a sneer. Someone pokes
me in the ribs. I see a raised footbridge
and begin to cross, the clouds already broken

up and lifting, the air brighter, richer.
I breathe deep, watch the light flow
around me. Even the temperature shifts,

cooler, yet it feels as if the sun had shone
there always. Along a narrow hall,
scenes of women dancing are frescoed

the whole white length of the wall.
"Did you paint this?" I ask a woman
suddenly there, her filmy dress and shawl

also like a dancer's. "It's in the wind's hand,"
she laughs, beckoning me to follow.
She takes me to another room, where music stands

are punctuation marks against the yellow
chairs, the pine-green rug.
Music is the subject. "Do you allow

strangers?" I ask timidly. A woman shrugs,
smiles, pulls me into her group.
They stand in a circle discussing Wagner

and *The Ring*. Carol is among them, her harp
propped beside her. I say, "I believe
I've been here before." She starts

playing, the sound of October leaves
swirling and falling. She nods. "The furniture's
been changed," she says. The others retrieve

their instruments and go. From above, a lecture
by one of the critics grows loud. "The quality
of an artist's work," he shouts, "can be measured

by the quality of the bargain he
makes with the devil." Outside, the ensemble
is tuning up. Someone strikes a key.

2

I remind myself how the dissembling
energy we spend our lives pursuing
slips away, shape-changer, resembling

Aphrodite or Cupid. We call it by elusive
names, but like the god who does not wish
to have his true name spoken, it whispers *Muse,*

promises to answer. Then, puckish,
it hides among oaks and vines. I study
its habits. Sometimes nocturnal, it's a dervish

who takes me for a partner in a leafy
cove, spins me to eloquence that lasts
until the moon grows pale, my muscles heavy.

But this is its brightest side, the fast
and frenzied sprite its best disguise.
What of the times it emerges after

long sleep, its thirst making it cry
for heartsblood, what of that legendary power
we consign to nightmare? What dies

when we deny it? How many hours
do I spend in the light, making the coffee,
attending meetings, classes, concerts, following

schedules? All the time, the *it* is again becoming *he*
who gathers me in when I'm low,
when my mind takes its sharpest turns, fleeing

safety, fleeing the marked, paved roads
for the gash in the grassy field, the ladder down,
half its rungs missing. I float

to the bottom. Slow. I leave the ground
of my being for as long as I can.
I want to see his face, know what I've found.

3

Saturday mornings I biked to Mrs. Mann's,
nearly always late for piano lessons.
Stout and saintly, my teacher never rapped hands

with a ruler, rarely chastened
with the metronome. I felt little shame for cheating
on my practice time. What I chose to listen

to and play were not the pieces
she assigned, cheerful melodies
evoking lacy dawns; I wanted icy evenings,

northern landscapes, threnodies
where every note fell labored, dark runs
and minor chords—tunes with more black keys

than my skills could navigate. I pumped
the loud pedal, blurred errors blissfully,
all *Sturm und Drang,* all thunder.

On the radio one Sunday, Mozart's *Dissonant
Quartet.* The introduction was all I needed.
I danced. From then on I insisted

all my music had to be diaphony,
until my teacher lost her famous patience.
When my parents let me quit, I'd succeeded.

Distance and time say it wasn't just laziness
and perversity. Like Tartini, I've dreamed
the devil in my chamber, curtains ablaze,

violins. He's not entirely what he seems
in paintings and the myths. Yes, passionate—
his cape and grin flamboyant. Yes, a fiend

who can entice a mother to murder her innocent
child, a man to fire a pistol into a crowd.
But what's less often seen is his intense

delight in what we do in the flood
of his love. There is another Angelus
that calls. We hear the loud

chime of its bell, a tritone Diabolus
in Musica. Trust what comes from below,
it peals. It speaks to me. It speaks to us.

4

How do we glide into our knowing?
What happens when we imagine the dust
we'll become? Can anything slow our dying?

A man lunches in a bright cafe, casting lustful
glances at the next table's lamb
and potatoes au gratin, at the woman who must

be dreaming there in the corner, her hands
clasped in her lap, head tilted
as if she listens to wind over sand

in some distant country, memory half silted
over. Somehow he already knows
that this is what their lives will be built

on. He imagines now that wherever they go
the past will live between them, sometimes
a cloud, sometimes a glittering show

that plays, with variations, in his mind,
a theater of reds and blacks. He is confident
that this is it: the world is not always kind,

but it's what we have—nothing radiant
waits on the other side. He's decided to garner
all possible joys, to plan the events

of his continuing, not to squander
the years ahead. He speaks to her.
And so it begins. Late, the two of them meander

out and down the vacant, narrow street. He burns
to say what it's too soon to speak of.
It *can* happen like this, though he's learned

no one trusts a man's sudden intentions in love.
Even he has always believed it's mostly glands,
no bolt of lightning, certainly, from above.

Whatever intuition is, it stands
in the shadows, rarely speaks in a man's voice,
we think. How much we fail to understand.

5

Are you the dreamer in the café? If so, what choice
do you have? Swept by events, by his ardent
promises, will you see this as fate? If there's a price,

when will you know it? Let's say you consent
to a voyage. You stop at a fishing village,
salt-battered houses, stores. There's been an accident.

A drowned girl has been brought in on a skiff.
She lies on the shore, the strands of her hair spread
in a sandy halo, her body rigid.

A crowd has gathered. Your lover buys bread
to feed the gulls. You want to find out
who she was, who loved her, what she said

before she left. He tells you this happens about
once a month. For people who live by the sea
and know better, he says, they're inclined to flout

safety. Look at their eyes. They're eager
to cast those slim bodies into the deep.
Sad, he says, but how it will always be

in these parts. You feel a sudden need to sleep.
He arranges your hair on the pillow, a fan.
In the morning, he brings coffee steeped

long, strong enough to wash the sand
from your eyes. By the time
you come home, you're wearing a wedding band.

And after that? It's true that we find
what we need. A darkness will prevail
in the evenings, when the restless mind

travels. You'll pick up a book, put it down, fail
to find the tape you want, play Robert Johnson,
then Paganini. Eyes closed, you'll see a plumed tail.

6

I'm in the South of France, in a train station.
When I round a corner, a man speaks, surprised:
What chance, to find you, of all places in creation,

here! *Do I know you?* I ask. I do not recognize
him. His hair is long, his face the face
of an angel. Then—those pale blue eyes—

I know it's John. His friend Jacob
is with him, and another man in clerical dress.
John (a composer) and I embrace.

The four of us find an English tea shop. Questions
fly at me: Do I remember the age
of Jesus at his death? I do. The tests

continue: Do I know a woman scholar of Donne? *At Yale,*
I say. With whom have I studied recently?
Jacob pulls out an ancient book, finds the page

he's looking for, nods emphatically.
The cleric, in a surplice with red trim,
a large wooden cross dangling

from his neck, says nothing. He rubs the rim
of his teacup with one finger, then leaves.
I remember John's faith: He is a limb

of the oak, the oak is God. Leaves
fall from him as radiant music, each note
a gift from the source, not himself. Belief

delivers him daily into his life. His open
face says it's still so. Nothing has ever shaken
that. His music swells with the passion

of his Lord. I recall once waking
to my words set to his song,
that plaintive music taking

me to a Xmas he diluted my wine with water, longed
to save me from myself. Though now we seem warm
acquaintances, something is clearly wrong,

the priest's silent departure a warning.
I know I've been judged
and found wanting.

7

Every clovered path leads to an under-
world where pomegranates fall from the fiery air
like manna. I bargain to come back up,

am startled to discover even the fair
winds of Rennes-le-Château blowing me toward
that contorted visage. The Church of Ste. Magdalen bears

these inscriptions: THIS PLACE IS TERRIBLE and LORDS
ARE BURIED HERE. At the entrance I find a devil
grimacing under a heavy vessel, hand minus its sword.

Lookout angels are poised above him, several
peering all directions but not at him or anyone else.
The painted Jesus crouches, positioned like the evil

one. In the countryside nearby, the lusty
devil appears in cryptograms—his hand, his breast—
and the rocking stones he rolled to the Place de la Coste.

He seems to be a familiar guest
of the village and in this odd house of worship,
where an ordinary sign reminds the visitor to rest

the yearning spirit. I remember the kinship
Jesus said exists among sinners.
Perhaps someone here understood his mission

better than I, a beginner
at deciphering these coded messages
carved in tombstones, scratched inside

pillars. Two centuries ago, priests found chests
of gold hidden by the Visigoths, the Templars,
the Cathars. But the real treasure

was in the secret graves: Jesus lived here,
it's believed, with Mary Magdalene, his bride and mother
of his sons and daughters. Oh, the kindling of fears.

The unacceptable must be *other*
in all its renderings. Curved horns, pointed ears,
insist *he* is not our brother.

8

Who is our brother? Who hears
us when we cry? Or when our child
cries? More to the point, the child dearest

to me, my own, the son whose wildness
as a boy, long-haired and drug-inflamed,
was not an ordinary break from the island

of the family, rebellion I could blame
on culture, the adolescent rage
that's like a fever. No, this was a maimed

child, whose mother came of age
too late, trading him for other loves and poems,
uncertain Art, a word-woven cage

of reds and blues she'd call her home,
inviting music in, and certain men.
This was my bargain. It left my only

child to wander west, to mend
as he could. All was not well.
Now he builds a house, sends

snapshots of it rising board by board. He sells
his labor cheap, dreams of making sculpture,
of re-creating himself. What do I tell

him? What do I tell myself? Can I nurture
him now that *he* is the age of Jesus at his death?
What does it mean, what conjecture

might connect the pieces? I read of the Earth,
the speculations of philosophers and physicists
about the stars, our place, the search

revealing order. Can a leaf, an eye, be chance? We insist
that it can, it is. And yet the odds deny
this cooled and rhymed universe. What if I stop resisting

that vast intelligence? How should I ally
myself? And what of chaos, that fiery friend
of artists? Does one truth make a lie

of another? Who's at the heart of us? What bends
like steel to belief? How do we make
ourselves artists, and to what end?

The sky explodes with light, and the ache
begins. I dream that my son makes sculpture,
weeping bronze heads, abstractions of wood and paper.

9

When my friend Moni is hired by an austere
American to sculpt Lucifer's image in marble and granite,
he thinks of Drac (Moni is Rumanian). His demon appears

to him, speaks his native tongue. A composite
spirit emerges—full, round breast on one side, penis
on the other, gorgeous plumed tail. It

stands now, all three tons, on the terrace
of a villa above Limoux, not far from Rennes-
le-Château. I try to catch a glimpse of the cultists

who live there. I take photos of Moni and his friend
as they install the piece, and of the gardens—purples
and reds, herbs—everything meticulously tended.

In the front the view is a grove of apple
trees and rooftops, the valley below
in mist. Off to the right a steeple

and the cemetery, huge silvery crosses a stone's throw
from the street. Moni welds the base
at the devil's feet. Sparks glow

in the air for minutes, rain into his face
and the devil's. Eyes unmasked, I'm entranced
by the light they make.

Later, on the radio, *Anitra's Dance.* Shall I dance
on the graves of my enemies? I wanted to say
Let me not, but the thought came out backward.

I wake with such urgency these days.
Music conspires again with dreams—
I watch a man and woman waltzing lazily

above the traffic, balanced on a beam
while construction workers pay no
attention, thinking, perhaps, the sweetness

on the air is accident. Liszt's *Consolation*
drifts from a window ten storeys up—
someone is practicing, repeats a phrase, slow.

*J'ACHÈVE CE DAEMON DE GARDIEN À MIDI POMMES
BLEUES.* (I DISPATCH THIS GUARDIAN DEMON AT NOON BLUE APPLES.)
Once more, Ste. Magdalen, a cryptic document. Light comes

through the stained glass at the south end stippled
so that at a certain hour, midday, a tree
ripples into focus, apples ripen red except

for three. Those three stay blue. Stevens'
blue guitar is strummed now by a demon who accompanies
a choir composed of deities

from everywhere. They sing off-key.
They hum Sibelius. They laugh together wildly.
They comfort me.

Note:

There are a number of mysteries associated with the village of Rennes-le-Château in the French Pyrenees. The Church of Ste. Magdalen there is a bizarre concoction of architectural and artistic puzzles, a result of its restoration in the nineteenth century by the abbé Saunière, who had come into unexplained riches. Images of the devil abound—in the church itself and in and around the village, which is believed by many to be the final resting place of Mary Magdalene, who according to legend was married to Jesus and bore his children. Some recent studies by scholars of the Dead Sea Scrolls seem to bear out the essential elements in the legend.